KEEPERS OF THE REEF

Written by
Dr. Sharon Wismer

Illustrated by
Alice Wong

TILBURY HOUSE PUBLISHERS

The oceans are vast, covering
our planet in a sea of blue.

In their dark, mysterious depths,
life is often hidden and out of reach.

Yet speckled across the **tropics**, like tiny oases,
lie underwater treasures far more precious than
those found in the shipwrecks of a time gone by.

In these clear, sunlit waters, life flourishes just beneath the surface on incredible living structures called **coral reefs**.

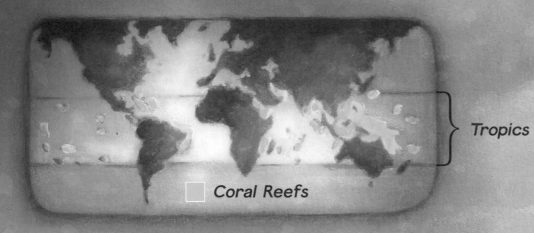

Tropics

Coral Reefs

Coral reefs are home to thousands upon thousands of animal species, including this sea turtle that lives on Australia's Great Barrier Reef.

When she's not basking on the beach or munching on sea grass, she spends her days gliding over her underwater kingdom.

Bright, colorful and teeming with life, coral reefs are the rainforests of the sea.

They cover less than 1 percent of the ocean floor, yet are home to more than a quarter of all the animal species found in the sea.

Would you believe that this magnificent structure is built by one of the smallest animals of them all? A coral **polyp**!

polyp

tentacle

skeleton

soft body

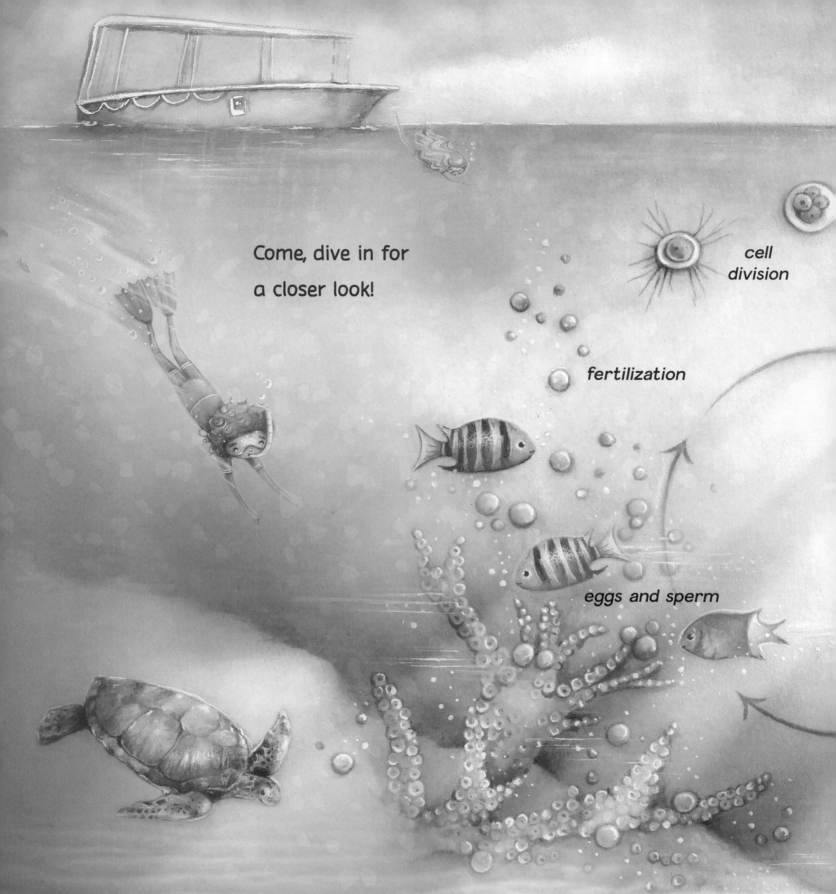

Come, dive in for
a closer look!

cell
division

fertilization

eggs and sperm

Polyps, surprisingly, spend the first part of their lives in the open
ocean, first as tiny eggs and then as free-swimming little **larvae**.

Tiny plant cells live in polyp tentacles and provide food to the coral. The plant cells and the animal both benefit from their partnership.

planula larva

polyp tentacles

zooxanthellae (plant cells)

settlement

coral
colony grows

Although they start out in the millions, only the lucky ones survive long enough to settle and fasten tightly to the **seabed**.

There, slowly, layer upon layer, polyps build a rocky skeleton, the hard foundation of a coral reef.

When polyps work together as a team, a **coral** colony is formed. Colonies grow in a variety of wonderful shapes.

A coral reef is formed when mound, plate, leaf, branching, finger, and other coral colonies grow together.

mound coral

plate coral

leaf coral

volcanic island

coral reef

branching coral

finger coral

encrusting coral

The **Great Barrier Reef** is the largest reef in the world. It is more than 2,000 kilometers (1,250 miles) long and made up of over 3,000 sections. This amazing structure is home to an incredible variety of life.

AUSTRALIA

Great Barrier
Reef

rays, sharks, reef fishes

sea turtles

snails, urchins, clams, crabs

reef-building corals

dolphins and
humpback
whales

Along with thousands of animal species, the Great Barrier Reef is also home to marine plants called **algae**. Unlike the single-celled plants that live inside the polyps, these algae grow on the reef, like plants on land.

Algae are a very important part of the reef ecosystem. They are the base of the reef's food chain and provide shelter for lots of tiny animals, including worms, snails, and crabs.

Turf algae look similar to grass and cover large parts of the reef. These short, thin strands often trap tiny sand and waste particles.

turf algae

Macroalgae grow big and tall, like bushes, and come in three colors: brown, red, and green.

macroalgae

Although algae are an important part of a healthy coral reef, too much algae can be harmful.

healthy reef

Without daily maintenance, algae can overgrow adult corals and make it hard for incoming coral larvae to find an empty landing spot.

reef after a phase shift

Over time, this can turn a beautiful, healthy coral reef into an underwater forest. This is called a **phase shift**.

Luckily, the Great Barrier Reef is home to a special group of fishes that help protect it!

Meet the **keepers of the reef**.

Bite by bite, day after day, these fishes keep algae in check and the reef healthy.

Working in harmony, every member of this keeper team has a job to do.

First up are bristletooth surgeonfishes.

These **brushers** use their special teeth to sweep up and remove the tiny sand and waste particles that become trapped within turf algae.

This cleaning service makes turf algae easier to eat by other members of the keeper team.

*lined bristletooth
(Ctenochaetus striatus)*

brusher mouth

By sweeping sand
away, brushers also
help corals survive.

bristle teeth ——

Too much sand casts a dark
blanket over the reef. That makes it difficult for
tiny coral larvae to find a landing spot and keeps
sunlight from reaching the coral's zooxanthellae.

After a good sweep, it's time for the **croppers**.

This mixed group of rabbitfishes and surgeonfishes includes the main grazers or biters of turf algae.

coral rabbitfish
(*Siganus corallinus*)

bluelined rabbitfish
(*Siganus doliatus*)

Croppers are like lawn mowers. They are responsible for keeping turf algae short, neat, and tidy. Without this cropping service, turf algae would grow bigger and longer, trapping even more sand.

Over time, unchecked turf algae could overgrow adult corals.

bluelined surgeonfish
(*Acanthurus lineatus*)

Small parrotfishes are called **scrapers**. Instead of biting, these fishes use their strong, beak-like teeth to scrape turf algae from old, dead corals, making little shallow clearings all around the reef. These feeding marks are landing spots for incoming coral larvae, helping the reef to grow.

jaw open, scraping

turf algae

surf parrotfish
(Scarus rivulatus)

three scraped clearings

coral larvae
in clearings,
ready to grow

larva looking for a
place to settle

sixband parrotfish
(Scarus frenatus)

palenose parrotfish
(Scarus psittacus)

Large parrotfishes are called **excavators**.

Like scrapers, they feed on turf algae, clear away dead corals, and create settling spots for coral larvae. But excavators leave behind deeper trenches while feeding, and even take bites of healthy, living corals.

bumphead parrotfish
(*Bolbometopon muricatum*)

By grinding up coral skeletons, excavators also help create beautiful, white sandy beaches.

By feeding on fast-growing coral species, excavators give slower-growing corals a chance to compete and survive. This results in reefs with a healthy diversity of coral species.

steephead parrotfish
(*Chlorurus microrhinos*)

Finally, **browsers** feed on large macroalgae. This job is done mostly by two species, the brassy drummer and the bluespine unicornfish. Together they ensure that macroalgae are a rare sight on a healthy reef.

Macroalgae, however, often bloom on coral reefs that have been heavily damaged.

brassy drummer
(Kyphosus vaigiensis)

When that happens,
browsers clean up the
weedy mess and help restore a
healthy balance between corals and algae.

bluespine unicornfish
(Naso unicornis)

Without browsers, macroalgae
would overgrow living corals and
crowd out new coral larvae, making
reef recovery nearly impossible.

As you can see, the health of the Great Barrier Reef is truly in the hands—or mouths—of its keepers.

Now, more than ever, the reef needs
this special team of fishes, as it faces
many threats and an uncertain future.

Local threats to the Great Barrier Reef include . . .

excessive and illegal **fishing**

physical damage from **tropical storms**

outbreaks of **coral-eating crown-of-thorns sea stars**

sand plumes from **dredging**

pollution from land-based sources

The greatest threat to the Great Barrier Reef, however, is **climate change**. Climate change is caused by the **burning of fossil fuels, factory farming**, and **deforestation**.

These human activities release **greenhouse gases** into the air, which trap heat from the sun.

Over time, this increases temperatures on land, and it also heats our oceans.

Corals do not thrive in hot water. When the water becomes too warm, corals begin to lose their zooxanthellae, the special plant cells living within their tissues. Without them, corals turn white as snow and slowly begin to starve.

This is called **coral bleaching**.

healthy   *bleached*   *dead*

If the water stays too hot for too long, bleached corals eventually die. This often destroys large sections of reef.

Such **mass bleaching events** cause too much destruction for the keepers of the reef to repair on their own. They need a helping hand!

All over the world, scientists have come up with clever ideas to help reefs recover.

In Florida, USA, **coral nurseries** are used to raise corals by the hundreds before transplanting them to a reef in need.

On the Great Barrier Reef, underwater **robots** help remove coral-eating sea stars.

And in the tiny island nation of the Maldives, in the Indian Ocean, there is even a man-made **3D-printed reef** for incoming coral larvae.

You don't have to be a scientist or travel to faraway places to help coral reefs. Turn the page for some ways to help from your own home.

protest for change

replace meats with plants

plant a tree

conserve energy

leave the car at home

look, but don't touch

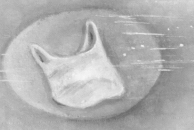

pick up litter

tell your friends

How can you help?

There are many ways to help the world's coral reefs, both at home and underwater. Taking steps to lower your carbon footprint is a great place to start. That means reducing the amount of energy you use by making small changes in your daily lives. Below are a few ways to do that. For fun, each action has a score.

Can you collect 10 coral points each month?

- Skip the car and walk or ride your bike instead (4 coral points)
- Plant a tree (1 coral point)
- Eat a plant-based food instead of a meat (3 coral points)
- Protest for change (5 coral points)
- Reduce energy use (1 coral point)

When visiting a coral reef, please always remember to:

- Only look and not touch (2 coral points)
- Pick up any litter you come across (2 coral points).

And always remember to share what you have learned (3 coral points). By working together, you can help the keepers of the reef protect the Great Barrier Reef, and coral reefs around the world, for many years to come.

Glossary

Algae are a group of aquatic and marine organisms that look very similar to plants. They range in size from microscopic to extremely large, like giant kelp. Like plants, algae use energy from the sun to produce food in the process known as photosynthesis.

Carbon footprint is the name given for the amount of carbon dioxide (greenhouse gas) that goes into the air because of a human's energy needs. Activities that use energy from fossil fuels such as coal, oil, and gas will increase a person's carbon footprint. This includes heating a house and driving a fuel-powered car.

Coral polyps are tiny, soft bodied animals related to sea jellies and sea anemones. For protection, they secrete hard, limestone skeletons, which form the foundation of coral reefs. When the skeletons of many polyps join together, a *coral colony* is formed. *Coral reefs* are created over many thousands of years when many different types of coral colonies grow together.

Greenhouse gases are gases in the Earth's atmosphere that trap heat, like carbon dioxide.

Larvae are animals in an early stage of life that occurs right after birth or hatching. Before becoming adults, larvae have to undergo huge physical changes. Coral larvae are called planulae and drift in the open ocean. Eventually they settle and attach to the seabed, where they change shape and grow into stationary coral polyps.

Mutualistic relationship is a partnership between two organisms that is beneficial to both. Corals (which are animals) and zooxanthellae (which are plant cells) are a great example of a mutualistic relationship.

Seabed is the ground or floor of the ocean. Coral reefs grow best when coral larvae attach themselves to the seabed in shallow, clear, warm water.

Species refers to a group of plants or animals that have similar features and are able to reproduce with each other. It is how scientists classify organisms into groups.

Tropics are the regions of the Earth located near the Equator. Warm and humid, they are home to coral reefs and rainforests.

Zooxanthellae are single-celled algae that live in a mutualistic relationship with corals. Like other plants, zooxanthellae photosynthesize. Harnessing energy from sunlight, they provide corals with nutrients. In return, zooxanthellae are given a safe living space within the tissue of corals. Zooxanthellae are also responsible for giving corals their many colors. Pronounced ZOH-zan-THEL-ee.

Further Reading and Resources

Berne, Jennifer, *Manfish: A Story of Jacques Cousteau.* Chronicle, 2015.

Chin, Jason, *Coral Reefs: A Journey Through an Aquatic World Full of Wonder.* Square Fish, 2016.

Earle, Sylvia, and B. Matthews, *Jump into Science! Coral Reefs.* National Geographic, 2009.

Lawrence, Ellen, *Slime Sleepers: Parrotfish.* Bearport, 2018.

Martin, Claudia, *Children's Encyclopedia of Ocean Life.* Arcturus, 2020.

Medina, Nico, *Where Is the Great Barrier Reef?* Penguin, 2016.

Messner, Kate and Matthew Forsythe, *The Brilliant Deep: Rebuilding the World's Coral Reefs.* Chronicle, 2018.

Munro, Roxie, *Dive In: Swim with Sea Creatures at Their Actual Size.* Holiday House, 2020.

Owens, Mary Beth, *Hawksbill Promise: The Journey of an Endangered Sea Turtle.* Tilbury House, 2019.

Rattini, Kristin, *National Geographic Kids Readers: Coral Reefs.* National Geographic, 2015.

Stewart-Sharpe, Leisa, *Blue Planet II (BBC Earth).* BBC Children's Books, 2020.

Weblinks

Great Barrier Reef Foundation
barrierreef.org/kids

NOAA: Coral Reefs
noaa.gov/education/resource-collections/marine-life/coral-reef-ecosystems

Roots & Shoots
rootsandshoots.org

Smithsonian: Coral Reefs
ocean.si.edu/ocean-life/invertebrates/corals-and-coral-reefs

Virtual Fieldtrips with the Nature Conservancy
nature.org/en-us/about-us/who-we-are/how-wework/youth-engagement/nature-lab/virtual-field-trips

Dedication

For Sophie, Julien, and Pearl-Lei—may you never lose your sense
of wonder and curiosity for the natural world. —S.W. and A.W.

Acknowledgments

We would like to thank Professor David Bellwood and colleagues for their years of scientific research and incredible discoveries. We would also like to thank GBRMPA and AIMS for educational resources; Professor Kimberly Nicholas and Dr. Seth Wynes, climate scientists, for their insightful comments; and the Swiss National Science Foundation for Sharon's postdoctoral funding. To our children and husbands, thank you for supporting our dreams. To the next generation (our readers), we hope to inspire and witness your future contributions; thank you for sharing our passion for the ocean and the marine life that lives in it.

Sharon Wismer is a marine biologist and co-founder of SEA Kids Alliance. From early childhood exploring tidal pools in Durban, South Africa, Sharon has kindled a deep curiosity for marine life and a passion for sharing its wonder and importance. Her doctoral studies at the University of Neuchatel, Switzerland, investigated the behavioral ecology of coral reef fishes, and her postdoctoral research at James Cook University, Australia, investigated the impacts of mass coral bleaching on the Great Barrier Reef. Her scientific work has been published in peer-reviewed academic articles in international journals. *Keepers of the Reef* is her first children's book, written and illustrated to make the emerging science of coral reefs accessible and exciting for children. Sharon lives in Switzerland with her husband and two children. You can find her at @seakidsalliance / seakidsalliance.com.

Alice Wong works in watercolor and pencil and has illustrated eight picture books and board books. Clients for her Beatrix Potter–style animal illustrations include Hallmark, Paperchase, Harrods, and many others.